PERSEVERE

—————— *for* ——————

PEACE

A Guide to Finding the Light in the Darkest of Times

JAMIE LYNN SOKOLOFF

Persevering for Peace
Copyright © 2020 by Jamie Lynn Sokoloff

Tellwell Talent
www.tellwell.ca

ISBN
978-0-2288-3923-1 (Paperback)
978-0-2288-3924-8 (eBook)

To my dad, Rick Sokoloff, who
left this earth way too soon.

May you rest in paradise.
I will make you proud.

Two percent of every book sale will go to Rick's Run, an event organization, founded by Jamie Sokoloff, that supports various charities throughout Canada in honour of Rick Sokoloff.

TABLE OF CONTENTS

per·se·vere

to continue in a course of action even in the face of difficulty or with little or no prospect of success. – www.dictionary.com

"After everything this year has thrown your family this year, you should write a book."

After hearing this for the 10th time, I decided to give it a try. What started off as a therapeutic exercise for me, turned into something far more beautiful than I ever imagined. I hope my healing journey through my year of grief, stress and heartache, brings you peace and inspires you to find the light in life. Life is full of horrible events, but we must find the light in order to carry on. We must get through tough times and learn to thrive through the pain.

CHAPTER 1

WHO AM I

These are the questions I am constantly asking myself: "Who am I?", "Why am I here?" The response to this is constantly changing but as of now, I am Jamie; I am currently twenty-seven years old and on the path of finding my purpose in life. Throughout my life, I have always been a nature lover and loved being outdoors whether it be lounging on the beach, hiking mountains, or going for walks. I love to be in nature; it is where I truly am my happiest and most connected to the earth. I love yoga, running, and experiencing new things. I am constantly changing, evolving, and growing. Every day is a new day and my constant desire for new experiences grows rapidly.

I have always had a passion of helping people and wanting to make a difference. After high school, I studied social work and gained over six-hundred hours of experience with children with Autism. I LOVED this. I loved seeing how differently those with Autism think and, honestly, some of the most amazing people that I have met in my life, were on the spectrum. After college, I was given a great opportunity at my dad's company as an education director and then took on the human resources role as well.

Although I was no longer directly "helping others", I did do other humanitarian acts. Every winter (to this day), I organize a clothing drive, collecting warm clothing donations and distributing these items to the homeless on the streets of Toronto. I have an amazing group of people who have jumped on board with this project every year. I have always found joy in helping others and have always loved organizing fundraisers. I have tried my best to be a good person and give back to the universe for the amazing life I have been given. I am not saying I do not have flaws, because I have a lot of them, but I am saying that I am trying to do better and help others who have not had the same privileges that I have had.

I am a born animal lover (and a new vegan!). I have two miniature dachshunds; Jax and Louie, a hedgehog named Holly, and a Tabby cat named Leo. I am working on getting a pig but have not won that battle yet with my boyfriend.

I have been with my boyfriend Jesse for six years. We have recently purchased our first home. We have gone through so much, travelled many places, climbed many mountains, drank too many beers in Ireland, rented a jeep and explored the Road to Hana, Hawaii, and stood behind a jet plane taking off from St. Maarten in the Caribbean. I could write a whole chapter on this part of my life! We have endured so many ups and downs over the years. The true test of any relationship is how your partner reacts when your life falls apart. You will read more about this amazing man in a few chapters.

I lived a privileged life; my parents always had money, and I always had new clothes. I have never experienced hunger or neglect. My parents were so full of love and supported me with anything I pursued. They had a big house, a pool, and always had new cars. Our life was very fortunate, and I thank my lucky stars every day for this. Making my parents proud was important to me. I lived to please.

My life has always been easy, and I do not deny my privilege in any way. However, when my life took a turn my amazing life was stripped away from me and I was forced to find myself again.

My view of the world changed drastically. At first, I hated the world and everyone in it. My perfect life had been taken away piece by piece and left a missing space in my soul. After a few months of soul searching, my view became lighter. I began to question my purpose and what I was brought here to do. Throughout this guide, you will see how my world crashed around me, and how I decided to see the light and walk away from the darkness.

My healing journey is neverending, and I will continue to evolve. I am so unbelievably grateful to share this journey with you, and I hope it brings you peace.

Who Am I – Self-Reflection

In order for you to obtain as much guidance on your healing journey, at the end of each section, there is space for you to reflect upon what you have just read. It allows you to apply this guide directly to your own life. This allows for self-reflection and allows you to really listen to your soul and determine which areas of your life need improvement.

Who are you? (Introvert/extrovert, career, age, spiritual beliefs, interests, family role, anything that outlines you as a person)

_____

_____

_____

_____

_____

_____

_____

_____

_____

_____

_____

_____

_____

_____

_____

_____

_____

_____

_____

What kind of person are you and what kind of person do you want to be?

_____

_____

_____

_____

_____

_____

_____

_____

_____

_____

_____

_____

_____

What are three things that light you up and bring you joy?

_____

_____

_____

_____

_____

_____

_____

_____

_____

_____

_____

_____

_____

CHAPTER 2

THE DAY MY LIFE CAME CRASHING DOWN

At age twenty-seven, my privileged world came crashing down, piece by piece. My parents were on their way to their dream trip to Bora Bora. For my dad's fifty-ninth birthday, they thought they would be eating room service on a balcony that backed onto their own private beach. The dream trip, backfired on their layover in Tahiti. My dad looked at my mom and said, "Kath, I feel like I am going to pass out." Then he collapsed and that is the last time she ever heard his voice.

It all started on a Wednesday morning, I was at my desk at work, feeling overwhelmed and on the verge of tears. I was unsure why as I did not have more work than usual. It turns out, my soul already knew about my dad on the other side of the world. I received a text from my dad's cellphone fifteen minutes earlier: "We have arrived in Tahiti, last stop Bora Bora." I was relieved, as you never know what can happen when flying. I always loved that my parents would tell me when they landed safely.

Then I got a text from my mom which said, "Our luggage didn't make it, but that is okay, we expected it not to as we barely made our flight."

Fifteen minutes later, another text, "Your dad is having a heart attack." I replied, "Why, because of the bags?" My dad was particular, so naturally, I assumed she was using a metaphor which so many of us use in a twisted way of explaining things. I wish he had been upset over the stupid bags. After a minute, I had the urge to call her. Turns out, it was not over the bags; the heart attack was due to a severe blockage in his artery called the widow maker.

He was resuscitated four times and clung to life as hard as he could. A couple waiting to board their flight jumped in and performed CPR until the ambulance came. My mom was in complete shock. My sweet dad was taken into surgery later that day to remove the blockage to his heart. My mom was stuck in Tahiti alone, without knowing a word of French. Her phone was her lifeline, her only support.

At that moment, my whole life collapsed. My dad, my mentor, my favourite person in this entire world was not going to recover from this. I ran from my desk into my dad's business partner's office and begged him to help me figure out what was happening. As I spoke to my mom, he wrote down the information so we could find out which hospital my dad would be taken to and other details. I'm not sure what came over me, but I needed to be calm for her. I told her to take a deep breath and to drink water. I told her I did not want to lose her and that my brother and I needed her. It took all my strength to not break down during this phone call. My brother Steve and my boyfriend Jesse also worked at the company, so somehow my brother came bursting through the doors and into the office to sit with me. He was at a meeting off-site but got to me in what felt like minutes. Shortly after, Jesse bursts in. With so much emotion in one room, all our hearts broke at once. Although hopeful, we knew what the outcome would be.

My mom spoke on the phone with us for a while but hung up to ride in the ambulance with my dad. Jesse and I left work and drove to my parents' house to see my aunt who lived in the basement apartment of their house. I was determined to find something to help my dad cling on to life. I dug around for the later-term ultrasound photo of my niece. He had been so excited to be a grandpa soon. I also tried to find the plans for my dad's dream home that was planned to start construction later that year. See, my dad had so much more to live for. My heart could not deal with the fact that he wouldn't be able to fulfill his dreams.

When we left their house, I called all my friends and family and let them know what was happening. I cannot count how many people had said I was in their prayers or that they would pray for me. I have never been one for religion, but at that moment in time I would take any support I could get. I believed in a higher power; I just wasn't sure what.

Jesse and I then drove to my brother's house, and he and I and our partners worked on finding a flight for my brother and I. We hoped we would be able to see my dad and convince him to hold on to life and fight through this.

After we booked our flights, Jesse and I went home. I jumped into the shower. Jesse had knocked on the door, crying hysterically, saying my mom was on the phone and I needed to get out of the shower immediately and take the call. I took the call, dripping wet, and my mom sobbed. My dad's organs were failing, she said, and it was time to say goodbye to him. She held the phone to his ear, I sobbed and told him I loved him and that I would make him proud. This was the worst phone call ever. How do you sum up your last words to your favourite person in the world?

That night, I prayed. I prayed to God and begged him to let my dad live. I didn't know if I even believed in him, but I thought it was worth a shot. I promised that I would believe and I would devote my life to him if he did this for me. I would never have another doubt again. I know now that prayer does not work like this.

I went to bed, crossed my fingers, and held onto the belief that he would survive this. I woke up many times and looked at my phone: no missed calls. I woke Jesse up so many times that night and said, "She hasn't called. He is still alive." I was so hopeful. At 2:35 AM on February 20, still February 19 in Tahiti, my phone rang. I thought if I didn't answer the phone, his death couldn't be true. I hesitated and asked Jesse to pick it up. He said he was sorry, but this was a call that I needed to take.

I answered it, and my mom told me that my dad had passed. His organs had failed. My mom had told him to go if he needed to go. She had held his hand while his soul escaped his body. At that moment, I knew I would never be the same again.

Jesse was hysterical. I had no idea how much my dad had meant to him until that exact moment when I saw his face when he heard the news. I stumbled out to my living room and dropped to my knees, crying and screaming, and feeling so lost. I told everyone I knew: family, friends, ex-friends, anyone who would listen. I did this until 4 AM before leaving for the airport for my heartbreaking trip to Tahiti.

Jesse and I picked Steve up. Jesse drove us to the airport and said his goodbyes to us. There was so much emotion in that goodbye, as we both knew that when I came back home, I wouldn't be the same person.

My brother and I walked through the departures area and waited in the line for the security check. I was so shaky, and my eyes were rimmed red from crying. When it was my turn to place my bag on the conveyor belt, I was shaking so much that I looked like I was guilty of something. I told the agent our father had just passed away. The agent looked at me and said how sorry he was for our loss.

Steve and I had never had an extremely great relationship, but on this day, it all changed. We cried together, we laughed, we bonded. All of this seemed like it was my dad's plan to get us on a plane together and support our mom during this terrible time. I saw a different side of my brother during this trip, one that made me honoured to be his sister.

After the long flight and layovers, filled with crying and memory sharing, we arrived in Tahiti. When we disembarked, I became hysterical. I took in our surroundings and realized this was the last place my dad had seen before he passed away. I was overheated, drained and so heartbroken. This was at the start of Covid-19, so we had to get our temperatures taken before going through to the luggage claim.

My eyes were rimmed red from crying so much; I knew everyone thought I was crazy. Who goes to Tahiti and cries when they land? A lady ran after us and said, "We have your parents' bags." I asked her how she knew it was us, and she said, "Because you were crying." She gave her condolences and said she had met my dad; he had spoken to her about his missing bags. She told us how infectious his personality and smile were.

After a few minutes, we took my parents' suitcases and went on our way. My mom had befriended a flight attendant named Helani who had seen my dad collapse.

She visited my mom at the hospital and brought her food and promised to pick us up at the airport. (Who knew angels were on Earth?) She held a sign, *Sokoloff.* She ran up and gave us the most genuine hug and loaded our bags into the car. She drove us to our mom's hotel.

My mom stood outside her hotel room on the second floor. Steve and I rushed up the staircase, Steve immediately ran to my mom and hugged her. I was still in shock, so it took me a minute to get to her. We hugged for what seemed like an hour. We didn't get much sleep that night, we just cried until we all finally drifted off.

I dreamt of Dad that night. He was skinny and frail, sitting in a chair. He looked miserable. He looked at me and said, "It's time to go…" I think this was his way of telling me that he died with his dignity and that is how he wanted it. He didn't want to get thin and frail and unable to take care of himself. He wanted his passing to go quickly and peacefully. He got that.

We woke up at 4 AM to the sound of hundreds of birds chirping, the most beautiful sound I had ever heard. We sat on the balcony crying and wondering what we did to deserve something so awful as losing him. After a few hours, we got ready and walked down to the hotel's restaurant for breakfast. Tahiti is such a beautiful place; it was a tease to be there under such horrible circumstances. At breakfast, we watched the waves crash and tried to eat our food. At this point we were numb; the food didn't taste like anything. I remember having some pain in my collar bone area, like I was carrying a heavy weight on my back. This was all too much for me to bear.

After breakfast, we went to the hospital to see my dad's body at the morgue. When I walked into that hospital, I swear my dad was in me. I felt strong and took the lead in making arrangements. I ran around the hospital, filling out forms and getting instructions on our next steps. I truly was not myself; I wasn't weak anymore, I was strong. This strength came out of nowhere and allowed me to do things I never thought I could do. I held back the tears and got what needed to be done finished. As we made our way into the waiting room to enter the morgue, I told myself I would not go in; I would stand outside while my mom and brother said goodbye. My last moment with my dad before he had left on his trip was a good one and I did not want to spoil that. My brother was not feeling well, like he was going to pass out. In my calm state of mind, I instructed him to breathe and not get up until he was ready. I knew I had to go inside and support my family. We went in and I said goodbye to the man who gave me my wisdom, who gave me my fortunate life. The last goodbye was heartbreaking; my dad, always tanned and full of life, lay there lifeless and pale as a ghost. His soul had escaped his body; he was not there. I found peace knowing he was in a better place.

From there, my strength multiplied, and I was able to get us to the funeral home where we made arrangements to get my dad's body home. We experienced some challenges along the way. Tahiti is a French speaking country, and our French was limited. We ended up needing my parents' marriage certificate, which, obviously, they had not travelled with. We pulled our resources together, using the help and support of others back home, and managed to get a form that was sufficient and got approval to have his body sent home.

We spent a few days in Tahiti tying up loose ends so Dad could make his way home to be celebrated the way he deserved. Those few days were devastating but also very beautiful. My family bonded and really leaned on each other and communicated in ways we had never done before. We spent time in nature, remembering how perfect our life had once been. Every morning, we woke up to hundreds of birds chirping. I believed it was my dad's way of saying we would be okay. We embraced the calm before the storm, as we knew when we returned home that our world would never be the same.

A few days before our lives changed forever, as a family, we celebrated my dad's birthday over dinner. We had been seeing each other almost every week for the past few months to celebrate birthdays, Christmas tree hunting, other Christmas festivities, and my sister-in-law's baby gender reveal. These past months we had met up more than we ever had before. I am so grateful that we all spent so much time together before his passing. The birthday dinner happened a couple days before we lost him. I had bought my dad a large canvas of a bear sleeping. He loved art, especially animal art. He loved it so much that I remember seeing his eyes light up when he opened it. He showed me exactly where he would put it. I was so happy he loved his gift. He and I talked a lot that night. I sat beside him while we watched *America's Got Talent*, his favourite show. We had such a great dinner, and I could tell he felt loved. It makes me so happy that in his last couple of days on earth, he knew he was loved.

The day my parents left on their trip they were at work until they needed to leave for the airport. When they told me they were getting ready to leave, my dad sat in my office and chatted with me while my mom tied up loose ends at work. He was so excited to tell me about their plans. He and I joked that my mom would have to pee right before boarding, which always seemed to happen. My dad asked me if I knew where his will was. (He routinely told me before they left for a trip.) I told him to shut up, jokingly, of course, and said I wouldn't need it, and that I would see him when they returned. I never thought I would actually need to know that information.

When they were ready to leave, something told me to give him a big hug. I felt sad they were leaving, which was strange because I loved that they enjoyed their lives together so much. I ran up and hugged my mom. Then I gave my dad a hug, and something told me to hold him a little longer. I told them I loved them and that I would take care of their French bulldog, Romeo. I remember my dad's big smile when he walked out the door. Our last moment together was a good one.

We finally arrived home after what felt like a month in Tahiti (it was only three days). We immediately arranged my father's memorial. We arranged for a beautiful service with a slide show of photos, and six speeches from my brother and I, a few work associates, and a few personal friends. I have never been a good speaker of any sort, but that day, my dad's strength came over me again, and I gave the best damn speech I have ever given. I honoured my dad, and I believe he would've been proud of me. The funeral home was overflowing; I could not believe how many people respected him. We estimated around 600-700 people were in attendance. My heart at that moment was full but also overwhelmed. This was a week before the state of emergency was declared due to Covid-19, so we do consider ourselves lucky that we were able to have such a big service before everything closed down.

After the funeral, I thought to myself, what now? What do we do from here? How do we keep living? Why do I want to go on without my dad?

After being up and down for a while, I hit the lowest point of my grief. I was angry and depressed and, quite honestly, questioned my existence and why I still needed to be here. I yelled at my boyfriend; I wished terrible things on him. I yelled at mom. I was nasty, and I hated the world. I hated work. I hated myself. I found no joy in life and did not want to move forward. I was a mess, and I am grateful to those who stuck by me when I was so awful.

After a while of being depressed, I decided to do some real soul searching and find a reason to enjoy my life again. This book is the result of my soul searching.

After deciding to live and enjoy life again and determining which changes needed to be made, I was struck with more devastating news. My mom was diagnosed with breast cancer. Could this year get any worse?

Two months or so after my father's funeral, my mom obtained a physical to get life insurance for herself. During a mammogram, she mentioned to the technician about a small lump in her left breast that her doctor had already determined was a cyst. After the mammogram, her doctor recommended a biopsy. Not thinking anything of it, she went for the biopsy.

The next week, she got a call from her doctor, who asked her if the breast clinic had called her yet. She said no but asked what was happening. She was told she had breast cancer. I was in complete shock when my mom relayed the news. Had we not been through enough? I was angry. Why was this happening to us? Why us? We are good people. Why did we deserve this?

My mom was shocked. She had never expected this, nor was she prepared for this! She and I went to her first appointment together. This was all during Covid-19, so we had to wear face masks to her appointment. The surgeon explained my mom's options, that she would need an MRI before the surgery would be scheduled. Due to Covid-19, the process took so much longer than needed as the surgeon was scheduled only once a week. My mom attended her MRI and waited for the results. It turns out she had another lump in her right breast and had to get another biopsy. This time, she was told that this lump was benign…better news. My mom sought another opinion from a doctor in Buffalo and had a virtual meeting to discuss options. The doctor from Buffalo pretty much agreed with her current doctor and said she would need to decide whether to get a mastectomy or lumpectomy. My mom decided on a mastectomy and had reconstructive surgery during the procedure. The surgery was successful but very stressful. My mom handled it with grace and worked very hard to keep a positive outlook. As I write this, she has recovered from surgery. She has a long way to go, but this will all be over one day soon, and we can move on from this terrible year. Her strength throughout this year has made me confident that she will fight through this.

This year has been one from hell, and it seems nothing had been going right; my entire world had been imbalanced without my dad. Everything I surrounded myself with has seemed to fail in some way. I soon realized I had been attracting negativity. I was part of the problem and also the reason things were not improving. I needed to gain control of my life, find peace, and a way to carry on without him. This book is a result of my journey for peace and self-development.

CHAPTER 3

WHY SHOULD YOU CARE ABOUT MY LIFE?

You may have read the previous chapter and said to yourself, "Yeah, that is a sad story and all, but why should I care?"

People tend to let go of things they think do not apply to them, and that is okay. The reason you should care is because I didn't give up. In the next few chapters, you will learn how I took my lowest point and created something beautiful. I taught myself to take life's worst moments and turn them into life lessons. I chose to honour my father and to carry his wisdom throughout my life.

You will also read how I chose the light and found my purpose. This book can (if you choose to listen) guide you into a happier, lighter, mindful life, no matter what you have gone through. Through my story, you will see how I climbed out of the darkness and made myself happier, stronger, and more positive. There is an opportunity to reflect upon each chapter and apply it to your life. This guide allows plenty of opportunities for self-reflection and will jumpstart your journey to self-development. The lessons I have learned from my dad are lessons everyone should hear at least once in their life. His wisdom was far beyond an average man's, and his advice and outlook on life needs to be shared with the world.

I vowed to myself to enjoy every day and to live for my dad.

Happiness is a decision and I choose to be happy.

<u>Write it three times in a row, and keep this line embedded in your head.</u>

Happiness is a decision and I choose to be happy.

CHAPTER 4

A LOVE STORY

Have you ever met a couple that was so right for each other and so aligned that it made you unbelievably jealous?

My parents were straight out of a love story. They did everything together: grocery shopping, cooking, haircuts, dentist appointments, you name it. They were so unbelievably right for each other. They fell hard for each other and showed it every single day. Together for fourty-three years and married for thirty-nine, their relationship was one of a kind. A relationship that I am so grateful I was able to witness or I never would've believed a bond like theirs was possible.

Watching them together filled my heart. Together, they built their dream life and enjoyed every minute. They travelled often, celebrated often, and were so generous to everyone. They drove up north to the cottage every

Thursday and didn't come home until Monday night. Together, they bought their dream yacht and parked it on the dock at their cottage. Their love was unconditional and irrevocable. The way he looked at my mom was something I will never forget. He loved her and everyone knew it. He spoke of her respectfully and supportively, never bitter.

My dad would always smile when Hedley's music video "Kiss You Inside Out" would come on. There is a scene where a couple falls in love at first sight. They get into a car accident and crash into each other and after that they fell so deeply in love that their lives were changed forever. Throughout the video you watch their relationship evolve and their love grow stronger. My dad always loved telling us that that is how he felt about my mom. They "crashed" into each other, and it was love at first sight. The second he met her, he knew his life was about to change forever. I never grew tired of this story. His face would light up and you could hear the love in his voice.

They met at a subway station. My mom was with a friend, and her friend walked into the men's bathroom by accident, right into my dad and his friend. After that, when my dad saw my mom and, his world changed forever. He needed to get to know her. He gave her his phone number. It took her three weeks to call him. She was playing hard to get. When she finally got the nerve to call him, they were inseparable. The rest of history. They moved in together, got engaged, had children, and their beautiful relationship continued to grow. They had nothing but their love, and they built a life around their relationship.

My parents were soul mates. They rarely argued and always spoke highly of each other. No matter how angry they may have been, they respected each other. Their relationship was built on true love and only got better with age. Their love was inspiring and almost seemed too good to be true. They dreamed together and built their life together. They were in sync, even with their parenting style. They never argued about how to parent us; they did it together. They had each other's back, no matter what.

My dad treated my mom like royalty; he wanted her to be happy. She returned that same amount of respect towards my dad. Their love story was unheard of. Because of them, I believe in true love. However, I also know true love, and a relationship like theirs takes years of growth and respect to achieve; it doesn't just happen.

My dad helped my mom fold laundry, load the dishwasher, and clean up after dinner. He was a man that women dream of. He helped my mom. They did chores together so they could finish the task quicker and enjoy more time doing the things they loved. My dad was present in their marriage and always picked her over everyone else. They truly enjoyed each other's company.

My mom was my dad's world; everything else was secondary. She made him happy and because he was happy, he was able to radiate happiness wherever he went. I truly believe that his happy marriage played a huge role. He was happy at home and had a life that he didn't need a vacation from.

My brother and I grew up with unconditional love and support. Our childhood was full of so many happy memories. Because my parents were happy people, they were able to show us how beautiful life could be and be positive examples for us. No parent is perfect, but my parents were pretty damn close. Nothing bad ever seemed to be that bad with my parents around. They were so goal-orientated that they continually came up with solutions to figure out any problem.

Their relationship worked so well. They complemented each other perfectly. My mom was the planner, and my dad went along with whatever she wanted. She was great with numbers and finances, and outgoing and trusting. He was street smart, responsible, good with people, and always on time. He was also cautious and looked at all angles of every situation.

My parents' relationship is one for the books, and I could probably write an entire book on them. Summing up thirty-nine years of marriage is hard to do, but the best way to describe their marriage is that it was strong, happy, and unconditional. They were so lucky to have found each other and to have experienced a love like this, and I'm sure my mom is grateful that the majority of their time together was spent smiling. True love never dies, and I know he will be waiting for my mom at Heaven's gates, smiling. Until then, the memories are forever, and my dad lives in them.

A Love Story – Self-Reflection

What does true love mean to you?

_____

_____

_____

_____

_____

_____

_____

_____

_____

_____

_____

_____

_____

Have you ever experienced unconditional love? From who? How did it make you feel?

_____

_____

_____

_____

_____

_____

_____

_____

_____

_____

_____

CHAPTER 5

MY DAD AND HIS WISDOM

My dad was a one of a kind man, the type most people do not get to experience in their lifetime. He had tanned skin, brown hair, and an infectious smile that was not easily forgotten. He was hard-working and always did what was fair. He was generous and invited others to enjoy his life's treasures. He was a simple man who did not like to stand out of the crowd, instead he chose to be humble.

He instilled a fierceness in me, one that I am still learning to manage. He encouraged us to strive for better and not take no for an answer. He was confident and knew what he wanted. He was a man out of this world and too good for this earth. He is with me always, everywhere; he is my moon, my stars, the wind. His strength has washed over me countless times since his death, and I honestly believe he walks with me.

He had an infectious smile. I loved everything about it. He radiated positive energy all the time. Even when he was upset, he still gave off nothing but positive energy.

My dad had a drive to be successful since he was young. He dropped out of school in grade 9, wanting to get into the workforce as soon as possible. In his day, dropping out was not uncommon; nowadays he would've been shunned. After my dad left high school, he immediately started working. His first job was at a toothpaste factory, putting the caps on the toothpaste tubes. He always had a job and always provided for his family, even when it was just him and my mom. He strived to do better and moved from job to job until he reached his goal.

My dad valued hard work and had so much respect for those who made an honest living and strived for success. He was a very intelligent man and had excellent business skills. He had a goal to start a successful elevator business, and he achieved this goal above and beyond what he ever expected. He started in the elevator business at the age of sixteen, working for his father. After a fallout with his father, my dad started his own business, RES Electric. From there, he reconciled with his father and bought his contracts from him and started Quality Elevator Technology, leaving RES Electric behind. He started out with only one other employee then grew his staff. Knowing he wanted to expand his business, he partnered with Allied Elevator Group, starting Quality Allied Elevator (QAE). Together, they grew QAE to become the largest independent elevator company in the Greater Toronto

Area. The family company became a multi-million dollar empire with over 120 employees. My dad was the heart and soul of the company and valued his employees. He led a family-styled business with a laidback environment.

Although successful, he never let it get to his head. He treated every employee the same. Another thing that stood out was the fact that he wore a work uniform to work. Never a dress shirt to show everybody that he was the big boss, never a tie. He wore the same uniform that all of his technicians wore. He said, "If I have to wear it, so do you." My dad took all the same mandatory training courses as his staff and never complained or felt too superior to do them. If anyone ever needed to talk, his door was always open.

I'm sure you have pieced together by now, that my mom was my dad's world. They were inseparable and did everything together, they were the image of true love.

When my dad became a father, he balanced work and family effortlessly. He worked hard to build us a beautiful life. He continually taught Steve and I life lessons and shared his wisdom. He was always so proud of us for our accomplishments, no matter how little or big, and proud of his family and the life he had built for us. He loved us so much, you could see it in his eyes when he spoke about us. I can honestly say, I do not have anything bad to say about the man. He trusted us, unconditionally. The trust he gave us made me afraid to disappoint him. This wonderful man trusted me, and I worked extremely hard not to betray that trust. He listened to us and did not react until he heard what we had to say. As deeply as I have reminisced about our relationship after his death, I now know that my dad did everything out of unconditional love. He was the type of man who was happy about the success of others. He was never jealous and never made others feel inferior. He was the greatest role model I could've ever asked for. I look back now, and I can clearly see that we were his life. As hard as my dad worked, throughout his life, not once do I remember him not being there throughout our childhood. He was always there, always available, and always happy to talk to us.

My dad was the type of person I could call no matter what. Once I called him crying when my boyfriend and I missed a flight home from Las Vegas (pro tip: airports use 24-hour time). He said, "Don't worry, you'll get home, calm down, shit happens." He and my mom proceeded to find us a flight. This is a memory he and I laughed about often. My dad was so calm while telling me that this would not be the last flight I missed and to stop beating myself up over it. He was always so calm and so understanding.

Another time my dad "rescued" me was while I was on a work trip in New York. A coworker and I travelled to New York City to attend a women's elevator group meeting. Our threeday adventure turned into a nightmare when our flight home got cancelled. We heard the cancellation was because of the weather, then we heard it was because of possible terrorist threats. I still don't know the full story, but something was going on! Panicked, I called my dad as I was supposed to have been in St. Lucia a couple days later. He promised me that he would help me get home one way or another. We proceeded to take a Greyhound bus home, the bus never came, and we had no explanation why. My coworker and I then tried to travel by train, but a train had derailed that day and no trains were going out. We called for a rental car and, of course, none of the rental cars were available. Hysterical by this point, I called my dad again. I was scared. He said to relax, check into a hotel room, and he would see what he could do. He ended up having a brilliant idea to call a supplier he used for business who happened to have a branch in Brooklyn. He called his contact and by the next morning, he had someone pick us up and drive us to New Jersey and rent us a car to get home. Once again, my superhero had prevailed and kept his promise to get me home!

When I was in college, I had a minor car accident: I smashed the front end of my car into a trailer hitch that caused my airbag to inflate. My dad was my first call. He wasn't mad at me; he was relieved to hear I was okay. He told me to take a breath, get out of the car and speak to the man I had hit. Again, he said shit happens and that this could've been so much worse. He calmed me down immediately, called a tow truck and called our insurance company. Within ten minutes, my dad had a plan for me to get a rental car until my car was looked at. I objected and told him I would never drive again. He told me this was not an option, and I would be driving a rental car as he did not want me to be afraid. Within an hour, I was in a rental car. He got his way. My dad always got his way.

When I was in grade 11, my parents bought me a cute little Jeep Liberty. I was so excited when I obtained my driver's licence! It took a few tries, but with my dad's help and guidance, I finally did it! The next month or so, I was driving myself to school and got pulled over for going 25 km over the speed limit. It was my first time getting pulled over, so I called my dad, crying. My dad said to breathe and ask the officer if he could speak to him. The officer said no, so my dad said, "That's okay, Jamie, call me when you are finished." Again, he was not angry with me whatsoever. He was calm. It turned out that I did not have my insurance or registration papers. The officer issued me three tickets, one for speeding, and the others for not having the correct documentation. I called my dad again and cried some more; he told me to relax and that shit happens. He told me to fight these tickets in court and that he would come with me. My dad and I attended my court appearance, and he spoke to the judge on my behalf. He explained I was just a kid saving for college and this would really hurt me financially. After reasoning with the judge, two out of three tickets were thrown out. My dad was very persuasive, and it was rare that he didn't get what he wanted.

The stories of my dad rescuing me and teaching me life lessons are endless. Throughout my life, he had been there for me no matter what. There was no question; my dad supported me no matter what. Our relationship in my twenties had developed into such a beautiful one. We talked often. I loved his stories, and I loved his smile; it was contagious. My dad had good energy, which made me feel good. He always encouraged me to do the right thing, to improve.

In my twenties, after college, I worked for his company part-time. I remember how happy he was when I decided to work there full-time. I asked him about getting involved in the education aspect of the business, and he was ecstatic. I remember his face when I strolled into his office and told him my decision. He was so proud of me. From there, I started my full-time position and climbed higher and higher up the ladder as I proved myself. Our relationship improved every day, and we worked on many projects together. Dad and I were both members of an elevator association that met quarterly. We would go together; my dad would drive. We would grab a coffee beforehand and talk about life, then we would proceed to the meeting. He was wellknown in the industry, and he knew everyone there. He proudly introduced me to everyone and told them about my job in the company. His face would light up when talking about me, my brother or my mom. I will never forget how he looked when he did. We would eat dinner at this meeting, and my dad would sneak another slice of pizza or cookie and say, "Don't tell your mom." Meanwhile, at home, we would laugh and tell her about it. These meetings meant so much to me, though I never expressed that to him; I hope he knew they did.

During my first meeting, my dad was thrilled to tell the members that his first meeting with the association was the day I was born! He told them how excited he was to have me there with him. That moment made me so happy he was my dad.

Every Friday around 11 AM, my dad would phone me. He always said he was checking on work, but I knew it was much more than that. We would start our conversations with work, but it would quickly change to personal life like our weekends coming up, what we were up to, how we were feeling, what we were looking forward to, etc., These calls always came, even when he was out of the country. I miss these calls more than anything.

I loved spending time with him. I loved listening to him speak, and I loved how much he loved me, unconditionally, and he made sure I knew it. My heart is still so full of love for him, and this relationship is one I will remember forever. His smile was my favourite part about him. His love of life was inspiring.

My parents loved to be at the cottage. The cottage was his favourite place in the world, and he would be overjoyed when my boyfriend and I would visit. My favourite memories are ones up at the cottage. He would cook some amazing meals and build us a huge fire.

My dad would always be cooking something on the BBQ, enjoying himself and ensuring that we all enjoyed ourselves as well. When my dad would have a couple drinks, he was still so happy, full of life, and so funny. I loved having drinks with him around the fire; it was so much fun. In the winter, we would all sit at "Rick's Bar," and he would play music videos on the big screen. He would play "Blurred Lines" by Robin Thicke. (Watch the video, and you will know why.) He would watch it over and over again. My dad had a great sense of humour. He was truly happy with his life; you could see it in his face. The cottage has been a real trigger for me, but I know one day I will enjoy it again and remember the happy memories we had there.

I miss him so much my heart hurts, but he is the reason I am pushing my journey of healing and self-development. This is all for him. If I could turn back time for one last conversation, I would thank him for my beautiful life and my memories with him. His legacy lives on through his family, and the memory of Rick Sokoloff will never die.

Here are a few life lessons that I have learned from my dad:

Persevere

This word was a part of my dad's vocabulary. When times got tough, whether in his business or in his personal life, he would always use the phrases "persevere" and "We will just keep persevering." These phrases have really stuck with me since his passing. I have "Persevere" tattooed in his handwriting on my wrist to remind me every day to keep pushing. This daily reminder helps me get my ass out of bed and move forward each day.

His happy-go-lucky attitude was admirable. No matter how bad things got, I could always count on my dad to lift my spirit. He would persevere through any situation and always kept his cool. He fought against all odds and made things happen his way. Whether the outcome was clear or not, my dad pushed through every tough situation and ended up on top.

This is by far the greatest life lesson from my dad. It taught me to live, to take risks and to stop living in fear of failure. Even if I fail, the goal in life is to keep persevering. When my mom was diagnosed with breast cancer, I told her we would persevere and fight. Life is worth fighting for, and sometimes it takes going through bad things to realize that.

What does it mean to you to persevere?

_____
_____
_____
_____
_____
_____
_____
_____
_____
_____
_____
_____
_____
_____
_____
_____
_____
_____
_____
_____
_____
_____
_____
_____
_____
_____
_____
_____

Get "thicker" skin

My dad often showed us tough love when we needed it. Whenever I was upset over something trivial and tried to get my dad on my side, he gave me his opinion whether I liked it or not. He would tell me to get thicker skin and not let my emotions get the best of me. As hard as my days have been since he's been gone, I truly have grown thicker skin, to help me get through the workday, to see a picture of happier days, to go to the cottage, to reminisce with friends. This life lesson has shown me how to live again and how to get through each day. My thicker skin does not mean that I have forgotten him; it means I am adaptable and remember him with gratitude.

How can you get "thicker" skin?

_____

_____

_____

_____

_____

_____

_____

_____

_____

_____

_____

_____

_____

_____

_____

_____

_____

_____

_____

_____

_____

_____

_____

_____

_____

_____

How can you stop letting your problems get the best of you?

_____

_____

_____

_____

_____

_____

_____

_____

_____

_____

_____

_____

_____

_____

_____

_____

_____

_____

_____

_____

_____

_____

_____

_____

_____

_____

_____

_____

Stop feeling sorry for yourself

In 2011, I had my first real relationship with a boy from high school. He and I were too young to know about love and too young to make our relationship work. As I had only seen my parents' relationship, which was always so in sync, I had unrealistic expectations for my own relationship. I would cry often and expect much more out of the relationship. Later, I learned that a relationship like my parents took years to develop and strengthen; it didn't take a couple of months. I was so convinced I deserved true love that I didn't think I needed to work on myself first. To this guy, if you are reading this, I am truly sorry for my high expectations, and I wish you the best.

After three years of expecting too much and being so disappointed, I was crying, and one day my dad came through the door. I would usually try to hide my tears but, on this day, I was just exhausted. He looked at me and already knew why I was crying. He looked at me and said, "Jamie, enough. Stop feeling so sorry for yourself and get your life together." I was immediately offended and walked away, even more upset. As I threw myself onto my bed, crying hysterically, I thought about what my dad had said. He was right; I was wasting my life feeling sorry for myself, when, in fact, I was the problem. All this time, I had thought my boyfriend was the problem. Turns out that I put my happiness into someone else's hands. To be truly happy means to be happy with yourself first. The next morning, I decided to call our relationship quits. It did take a few months to be officially over, but I had made up my mind.

Although I wasn't single for long, I took time for myself and worked on self-improvement. This time to myself led me to meet the love of my life, Jesse. Although our relationship is strong most of the time, I often use this advice to remind myself that a relationship works two ways. Rather than blaming my partner (which I am still guilty of sometimes), I need to look inwards and focus on a solution.

I realize now that all my dad ever wanted was for me to be happy. He wanted me to grow and focus on the positive and to move forward. So, I decided to stop feeling sorry for myself and move forward. My dad's advice led me to a lifetime of happiness with my partner.

Have you ever put your happiness into someone else's hands? How can you make yourself responsible for your own happiness?

_____

_____

_____

_____

_____

_____

_____

_____

_____

_____

_____

_____

_____

_____

_____

_____

_____

_____

_____

_____

_____

_____

_____

_____

_____

_____

_____

_____

_____

_____

The rain will pass, and the sun will come out again

My dad was a boater. He had recently bought his dream boat, a gorgeous 52 ft. Carver. He was always happiest when he was on the water. Some of my best memories with my dad were on the boat. Whenever we had planned to spend the day on the lake, and it rained, my dad would look at me and say, "The sun will come out again." This has stuck with me. No matter how rainy of a day it is, the sun will come out eventually. I think we all need to embrace the fact that no matter how difficult your life is right now, the sun will shine; you we just have to push through the darkness. My favourite memories of my dad include sunny days out on the boat. Although we had some rainy days, my heart remembers the sunny ones the most.

Was there a time when you felt things would never get better? How did they ultimately improve?

_____

_____

_____

_____

_____

_____

_____

_____

_____

_____

_____

_____

_____

_____

_____

_____

_____

_____

_____

_____

_____

_____

_____

_____

_____

_____

_____

_____

Exercise: On a rainy day, write down all of the things you love about the sunshine, and before you know it, the sun will be shining and you will be in gratitude.

I love the sun for it's warmth.

I love running in the sun.

I love sunbathing.

I love......

If you can dream it, you can do it

My dad lived his dream life with my mom at his side. He had a successful business, a happy marriage, responsible and independent children, his dream boat, his dream cottage, and everything in his life was perfect. He built the life of his dreams and enjoyed every day of it. He always told me, "If you can dream it, you can do it."

He taught me that no dream was too big and if I wanted something bad enough, then I would achieve it. He taught me to dream and use my imagination. I believe my father used the Law of Attraction to create his dream life. He thought positive thoughts and always strived to make things happen. If there is an afterlife, my dad is living the life of his dreams and waiting for his family to join him. One day, Daddy, one day we will meet again; until then, I will keep your legacy alive and keep dreaming.

What are your dreams?

_____

_____

_____

_____

_____

_____

_____

_____

_____

_____

_____

_____

_____

_____

_____

_____

_____

_____

_____

_____

_____

_____

_____

_____

_____

_____

_____

How can you make them happen?

_____
_____
_____
_____
_____
_____
_____
_____
_____
_____
_____
_____
_____
_____
_____
_____
_____
_____
_____
_____
_____
_____
_____
_____
_____
_____
_____

Work hard but enjoy your life even more

Hard work was something my father took seriously. As you know from the opening of this chapter, he worked hard his entire life to build his company into the success it is now. He worked hard to provide for my mom, brother, and me. He worked hard to raise us to value hard work.

Although my dad worked hard and had his cellphone on 24/7, he played even harder. He enjoyed his life and everything in it. He enjoyed the cottage, fishing, boating, and travelling with my mom. They travelled a few times a year, went out boat trips a few weeks each year and spent time at their cottage, which my dad referred to as his Northern Office. My dad enjoyed entertaining and cooking for his guests. My parents were generous and always welcomed friends to their cottage with open arms. He truly enjoyed every day of his life. He was happy to share his life's treasures with others.

My dad knew how to balance his life. Balancing working hard and living his best life was an aspect that he had mastered. He showed me that although hard work is important, enjoying your life was even more important. My parents never waited to enjoy their life like so many people do. Most people wait until they are retired, until they have lost weight or until their kids have grown up. My parents didn't wait; they balanced working hard with enjoying their lives.

This lesson is so important. My dad taught me to create balance. He taught me to have fun now and enjoy my life every single day, as we never know how many more days we have on this earth. He taught me to live life and to stop waiting.

How can you create balance in your life?

_____
_____
_____
_____
_____
_____
_____
_____
_____
_____
_____
_____
_____
_____
_____
_____
_____
_____
_____
_____
_____
_____
_____
_____
_____
_____
_____
_____

What have you been waiting to do? What is holding you back?

_____

_____

_____

_____

_____

_____

_____

_____

_____

_____

_____

_____

_____

_____

_____

_____

_____

_____

_____

_____

_____

_____

_____

_____

_____

Always be confident and don't worry about anyone else's opinion of you

Whenever my dad entered a room, he lit it up. His extraordinary confidence meant he could speak up whenever he wanted and the entire room would listen to him. You could sense his confidence and security within himself whenever he was close to you. He never needed reassurance from anybody. He never worried about anyone else's opinion of him.

The confidence he portrayed is why I looked up to him so much. He taught me on multiple occasions that others' opinions didn't matter. All that mattered was how you felt about yourself. My dad constantly pushed me to speak up and get over my insecurities. Confidence is such an important aspect of living a successful life.

This lesson is something I need to work on still but one I keep in the back of my head.

How can you be more confident and secure with yourself?

_____
_____
_____
_____
_____
_____
_____
_____
_____
_____
_____
_____
_____
_____
_____
_____
_____
_____
_____
_____
_____
_____
_____
_____

Make traditions

My dad was a huge believer in keeping traditions. He loved being with his family and celebrating together. He honoured our family traditions and ensured we kept them alive each year. He believed making traditions kept the spirit of those we had lost alive. This belief resonates so much with me as I plan to continue with our traditions and keep his spirit alive.

Christmas was by far my dad's favourite holiday. Every Christmas our family would cut down a Christmas tree together. Even as my brother and I got older, we kept this tradition going. It later turned into us taking a shot of fireball whisky to keep warm as we picked a tree. We would then go back to my parents' place, eat a nice dinner and decorate their tree together.

My dad and I would Christmas shop for my mom every year during the first week of December. We would be sent to the mall with a list of ideas for my mom that she put together to make shopping a little easier for us. He and I would have so much fun shopping together and catching up on each other's lives. I loved this time we spent together. After shopping, he and I would go to the food court for Greek food. Once home, I would take the gifts into my room and wrap them for my dad. This tradition he and I shared will be what I miss the most.

Every Christmas Eve, my parents would make a veal dinner with German potato salad, in honour of their close friend Bonnie whom they had lost. Bonnie was German and used to invite my parents over for Christmas Eve dinner. After she passed, they incorporated this German meal to their own Christmas Eve dinner at their place. We would have my mom's sister and her son over, as well as my Grandma before she passed away. After dinner, we would go downstairs to their Christmas tree and exchange gifts. We would watch a Christmas movie and usually talk over it. When Steve and I were young, we would get a Christmas Eve gift: always new pyjamas. No matter how many times they tried to trick us, we always got pyjamas. Christmas morning would consist of me waking everyone up far too early, and everyone moaning and groaning but getting out of bed anyways. Coffee was a must before opening presents. When we finally got to open gifts, we would start with our stockings, stuffed to the brims with small gifts. Our Christmas' were always so amazing. My parents put so much effort into making us feel special.

These traditions kept our family close and gave us an excuse to spend time together. My dad put these traditions in place, in hopes that my brother and I would continue them for the remainder of our lives. My dad was a family man and traditions with his family meant the most to him. I will always remember his smile on Christmas Eve at the dinner table. He was so proud of us all.

I am unbelievably grateful for these Christmas mornings. These memories will stay in my heart forever. Traditions are so important for families to create. I will keep these traditions that my dad set out for the rest of my life to keep his spirit alive.

What traditions do you have? What traditions would you like to create?

_____

_____

_____

_____

_____

_____

_____

_____

_____

_____

_____

_____

_____

_____

_____

_____

_____

_____

_____

_____

_____

_____

_____

_____

_____

_____

_____

_____

_____

How can you honour those you have lost and ensure their spirit stays alive?

_____

_____

_____

_____

_____

_____

_____

_____

_____

_____

_____

_____

_____

_____

_____

_____

_____

_____

_____

_____

_____

_____

_____

_____

_____

_____

_____

What traditions would you like to leave behind for your family?

_____

_____

_____

_____

_____

_____

_____

_____

_____

_____

_____

_____

_____

_____

_____

_____

_____

_____

_____

_____

_____

_____

_____

_____

Take a step back

When faced with a decision, my dad would tell me to take a step back. "Take a step back and weigh your options. Digest the information and take a few moments to think about it." My dad was wise beyond his years and mastered the art of thinking before he spoke. He also advised this when angry, or in an argument with someone. He taught me that sometimes you can't take words back, and it is best to take a step back and gain your composure. Avoid any sudden decisions.

How can you remember to take a step back when faced with a decision?

Digest

As mentioned earlier, my dad would often take time to digest information before jumping to a decision. He always took the time to weigh the pros and cons of every situation. When information was presented, and a decision needed to be made, he would say, "Let me digest this, and I will call you later." He was never intimidated but ensured he fully understood the situation before making any sort of agreement. He took time to think and never let anyone force him into a decision he was not comfortable with. I often find myself needing time to digest information before committing to anything. I learned to take my time and think about things and not let others' opinions sway me. This is a life skill needed in business but also in personal life.

How can you digest information before making decisions?

_____
_____
_____
_____
_____
_____
_____
_____
_____
_____
_____
_____
_____
_____
_____
_____
_____
_____
_____
_____
_____
_____
_____
_____
_____
_____

Put your blinders on

This is an especially important lesson, especially in business. My dad had over 100 employees, some of whom tested their limits such as taking long lunches, making personal calls, filling up with gas for the weekend, and leaving early. Others would bring these issues to his attention, and he would say, "Put your blinders on," meaning we should pick our battles wisely. If an excellent employee takes a forty-five minutes lunch instead of thirty minutes, that does not make them any less valuable. He never nickeled and dimed anyone, and he gave everyone the benefit of the doubt. He valued his employees and did not cause a fuss over trivial things. By no means did he allow them to take advantage of him; rather, he picked his battles wisely and dealt with only those things that needed to be addressed (unsafe work, excessive time off, time theft.) He put his blinders on for trivial things, even as Steve and I were growing up. He would never lose his temper with us it was something important. He was a very fair man who never gave anyone shit who didn't deserve it.

How can you "put your blinders on" and not let trivial things get to you?

_____

_____

_____

_____

_____

_____

_____

_____

_____

_____

_____

_____

_____

_____

_____

_____

_____

_____

_____

_____

_____

_____

_____

_____

_____

_____

_____

Do not get attached to material things

Throughout my life, my parents would buy new cars, new boats, and other new things. I remember my dad getting a new truck and being excited to show me all the new features. Once, in the back of his new car, I asked him, "Don't you ever miss your old trucks?" He looked at me and smiled and said, "Jamie, never get attached to material things. There is always something better out there." My dad never got attached to clothing, cars, even his boats. He would strive for better and enjoyed things while he had them but let them go when something better was in reach. He never let the sentimental value of material items hold him back. He was a simple man yet so wise beyond his years. He taught me that material things do not matter; it was the people you loved who did. Never greedy, he shared his things with the people he loved.

What material things do you need to let go of? What things are you holding on to that no longer serve you?

_____

_____

_____

_____

_____

_____

_____

_____

_____

_____

_____

_____

_____

_____

_____

_____

_____

_____

_____

_____

_____

_____

_____

_____

_____

_____

_____

Live life without regrets

This life lesson is one I strongly believe in. My dad never had regrets for his actions; he stood by his decisions and did not act until he had taken time to think them out. His relationship with his siblings was perpetually rocky, but he never regretted anything. He never let anyone's negativity influence his decisions. He never regretted starting his business. He never regretted marrying my mom and starting a family, and I'm sure he never regretted enjoying his life and well-earned money. I believe you must put your whole heart and soul into everything you do and not let anyone bring you down. Learn from your mistakes but never regret your past; use them to perfect your future. Weigh your decision beforehand to ensure it is the best one for you. Do not let regret hold you back from living your best future. I can honestly say I have no regrets with my father. I spent as much time with him as I could, and I respected him. As a teenager, I wasn't exactly the friendliest in the world, but I have never regretted those days that shaped my adult relationship with him.

How can you ditch your regrets and learn to move forward and live your best life?

_____

_____

_____

_____

_____

_____

_____

_____

_____

_____

_____

_____

_____

_____

_____

_____

_____

_____

_____

_____

_____

_____

_____

_____

_____

_____

_____

See the big picture

This was my dad's number one rule in business. He never let trivial things affect him; he seemed to see the big picture and envision where he wanted to be. He never got upset over minor setbacks as the outcome was so clear to him. He was calm and focused on what he wanted to happen. When I would get upset over trivial things such as someone talking over me in a meeting, he would tell me to see the big picture; small things did not matter when an outcome is clear in your mind. He wanted me to think about what I wanted and come up with a plan on how I would get there. Speed bumps along the way were inevitable, but they never got in the way of an end goal that was so clear in his mind.

How can you learn to see the "big picture?"

_____

_____

_____

_____

_____

_____

_____

_____

_____

_____

_____

_____

_____

_____

_____

_____

_____

_____

_____

_____

_____

_____

_____

_____

_____

_____

_____

What does your "big picture" look like? Where do you want to be?

_____
_____
_____
_____
_____
_____
_____
_____
_____
_____
_____
_____
_____
_____
_____
_____
_____
_____
_____
_____
_____
_____
_____
_____
_____
_____

A deal is a deal…is a deal

My dad was a man of his word. He never let people down, and a promise was always a promise. When my dad promised me something, I knew he meant it. I remember when I was little, my dad taught me the importance of keeping your word. He would say, "A deal is a deal…is a deal." That is drilled into my head, and I now value the importance of keeping my word. I never commit to anything I don't intend to keep. If I'm not sure about something, I will tell the person that I will get back to them. I never break a deal unless I have a damn good reason. My biggest pet peeve is unreliable friends who commit to things that they truly have no intention of doing. I have had a few of those people come and go in my life. Those who commit to things and complete them are my kind of people!

Do you keep your promises? Do you commit to things you do not plan to do?

_____

_____

_____

_____

_____

_____

_____

_____

_____

_____

_____

_____

_____

_____

_____

_____

_____

_____

_____

_____

_____

_____

_____

_____

_____

_____

_____

_____

CHAPTER 6

TRUE COLOURS

When times get tough, people's true colours shine right through. I have had the opportunity to see this first-hand. In moments like what I have gone through, you find your people and determine who your soul feels good around. Unfortunately, you also see the toxic people. Determining and excluding the toxic people in your life is the best way to clear your life of negative energy. Finding your people makes it easier to find the light. My people make me feel good and support me regardless of what I decide to do. They call me out when I am wrong and encourage me to do better. They are solid and reliable and there through it all. My people treat me how I would treat them. You are who you hang around, so make sure you are surrounded by people who make your heart happy. Sometimes life works in mysterious ways and allows you to see people for who they really are.

Find Your People

My friends

I have had so many friends throughout the years, but the ones that were there for me will be my friends for the remainder of my life.

A friend I hadn't spoken to in two years, due to a dispute, stepped up to the plate. She told me that we would deal with our issues later and that she wanted to be there for me during this time. We still have yet to deal with our issues, but our relationship has just gotten stronger.

I had my vegan friend, who visited me with trays and trays of healthy food after my dad had passed. She stood by me and gave me her strength when I didn't have any. We have been friends since I was eight, and she did not disappoint when I needed her.

There was my spiritual health-conscious friend who healed me and taught me how to heal myself. She constantly checked in on me and listened to me cry and vent on numerous occasions. She offered support when I simply needed someone to talk to.

I had my cousin in Ireland who has been a friend to me throughout all of this with her constant check-ins and emails. She was my first call after I got the call from my mom saying that my dad had past away. It was already late morning for her in Ireland, so she picked up my facetime call right away. We cried together, she comforted me. I felt her love and compassion for me through the phone. I will never forget how present she has been in my life, even know she is thousands of miles away! She is one of a kind, and I am very grateful for her.

I also had a new friend whom I met last summer at her wedding. My boyfriend's good friend had moved to BC and met the girl of his dreams. This beautiful soul lives on the other side of Canada but has made herself and her positivity so present in my life.

These women helped me so much in their own ways, and I will never forget it. I have received unconditional love and support and I am forever grateful.

My boyfriend

My boyfriend Jesse has been the most supportive, comforting person to me. He has given me a lot of space and picked me up off the floor when I was too weak to pick myself up. He has encouraged me to follow my passions and encouraged every lifestyle change I have ever made. I was not the easiest person to love, and he loved me anyways. He loved me no matter how angry and mean I got, no matter how difficult I was. He showed me that he would be there whenever I needed him but would also allow me to heal however I needed to. He accepted me when I became vegan, when I spent days in bed crying, when I organized a 15 km run. Anything I wanted to do, he supported, no matter how crazy it seemed.

He loved my dad so much; I will never forget the look on his face when he heard the news of my dad's passing. When my brother and I left for the airport to meet my mom in Tahiti, he woke up at 4 AM and took us to the airport. While I was away in Tahiti, he did all the laundry, grocery shopping, and cleaning, and even had my mom's room at our house set up with a TV. He also brought my mom's dog when he picked us up from the airport. Anything I needed, he was there. My boyfriend's colours shined during this mournful time, and I do not give him enough credit. He is my person, and I am incredibly lucky to have him. I see a future with him full of joy, love, and laughter.

My brother

Steve and I have never been super close in our adult life, but what happened to us changed everything. (As kids, we were closer, but he is five years older than me, so we were constantly at different stages in our lives.) After our dad passed away, we bonded like we never had before. I saw him in a different light and determined that he is so much like our dad. He is a great husband and an absolutely amazing dad himself. When he called my mom and me to tell us that his wife had given birth to their baby girl, he was ecstatic. He was so proud to show her off to us. Seeing him with his daughter reminds me so much of how my dad used to be with me. My brother has been my rock these past couple months. I can cry to him, I can bitch to him, and no matter what I have to say, he listens. If he doesn't agree with me, he tells me straight. He makes me feel like my dad used to, like I can accomplish anything in the world. His encouragement means he truly wants the best for me. Our dad would be so proud of him for stepping up and supporting my mom and me, and for being the best damn dad he can be to his baby girl.

My mom

My mom is one of the strongest people on this planet. Her life before she met my dad was terrible. She had lived in poverty, lost both of her parents at a very young age, and had extremely bad luck. Her luck changed when she met my dad. They built a life of their dreams together. Losing her husband after thirty-nine years of marriage was devastating for her. Her strength through all this is admirable. She chose to live for my dad and try the best she can to enjoy the life he had created for her. After being diagnosed with breast cancer, she was still so strong. After a moment of sadness, she would pick herself up and fight for her life. She would look at the bright side and remain positive. As I write this, she is at the beginning of her treatments, but I can say, without a doubt, she will kick cancer's ass and live the rest of her life in gratitude and positivity. I knew my mom was a strong woman, but this experience has made me see her in a different light. She is not only strong but a beautiful, generous, and loyal person. I am so grateful to have her, and I know my dad is looking down with a smile on his face.

Cutting Ties

Family may mean blood relations, but that is about it. The majority of my family throughout this tragedy have been the worst. Although there are a select few relatives on both sides that I have turned to and leaned on, there are also a few who have shown their true, nasty colours. Some family members have been jealous of my dad's success and never tried to hide it. Although most of them attended the funeral, we have not heard from them since. Not one call, not one text, just silence. I have now decided to rid myself of them and cut ties. When you finally decide to cut all ties, you become free of negativity. Anyone (family or otherwise) who is not there for you on your darkest days does not deserve you on your bright ones.

I have also determined who my true friends are and rid myself of fairweather friends. Friends who are only there when they need something are not true friends. To determine that is a huge part of healing. Freeing yourself of anyone who doesn't bring you joy is a very liberating experience.

Determining the good areas in your life is the best way to heal. If you focus all your energy on the good and hold them closely, the positivity creeps over you. Cut ties with those who do not make you feel loved. Anyone who does not hold your hand through tough times is not worth holding on to. Freeing yourself of negative influences is the start of your healing journey.

Cutting Ties — Self-Reflection Exercise

Is there someone in your life who makes you feel bad about yourself?

_____

_____

_____

_____

_____

_____

_____

_____

_____

_____

_____

_____

_____

_____

_____

_____

_____

_____

_____

_____

_____

_____

_____

_____

_____

_____

_____

_____

Is there someone in your life who only comes around when they need something?

_____

_____

_____

_____

_____

_____

_____

_____

_____

_____

_____

_____

_____

_____

_____

_____

_____

_____

_____

_____

_____

_____

_____

_____

Is there someone in your life who does not support your decisions?

_____

_____

_____

_____

_____

_____

_____

_____

_____

_____

_____

_____

_____

_____

_____

_____

_____

_____

_____

_____

_____

_____

_____

_____

_____

_____

Why are these people still in your life?

_____

_____

_____

_____

_____

_____

_____

_____

_____

_____

_____

_____

_____

_____

_____

_____

_____

_____

_____

_____

_____

_____

_____

_____

_____

_____

How can you cut ties with those who do not bring you joy?

_____

_____

_____

_____

_____

_____

_____

_____

_____

_____

_____

_____

_____

_____

_____

_____

_____

_____

_____

_____

_____

_____

_____

_____

_____

_____

_____

True Colours — Self-Reflection Exercise

Who are your people?

_____
_____
_____
_____
_____
_____
_____
_____
_____
_____
_____
_____
_____
_____
_____
_____
_____
_____
_____
_____
_____
_____
_____
_____
_____
_____

Who motivates you to do better but supports you no matter what?

_____

_____

_____

_____

_____

_____

_____

_____

_____

_____

_____

_____

_____

_____

_____

_____

_____

_____

_____

_____

_____

_____

_____

_____

_____

_____

_____

_____

_____

Who does your soul feel good around?

CHAPTER 7

HOW TO LIVE AGAIN

After my life crumbled down around me, I had to make a change. I had two options:

I could give up on life and feel sorry for myself.

OR

I could choose to be happy and use my experiences for good.

I chose to be happy and use my negative experience to help people and to live again for my dad. I chose to share his wisdom with the world. In order to choose happy, I had to make changes in my life. I was very fortunate that my partner was supportive of my life changes and accepted them with open arms, but I needed to make changes regardless of anyone's opinion. The changes were extreme but changed my life for the best.

To move your life in a positive direction, you have to be willing to change. You need to fully commit to doing better. Here are a few life changes I made to achieve this.

Find something that makes you happy

I took a deep look at my life and realized that I rarely did anything that made me truly happy. I vowed to do one thing a day to make myself happy from a list of simple things. I had written down gardening, plants, pets, animals, being outside, reading, being at the water, travelling, pets, natural products, and many other simple pleasures!

My boyfriend and I had moved into our first home in October, four months before my life took a terrible turn. Our backyard was tiny but gorgeous, with only one small garden patch. In May, my boyfriend dug up two more gardens, giving me tons of space to create the gardens of my dreams: herb gardens, vegetable gardens, and tons of flowers. I am honestly so grateful for him; I do not give him enough credit (it also doesn't hurt that he is a handyman!). Every day (weather permitting as we do live in Canada!), I start my day by watering my plants and checking for new growth. I also do this when I get home from work. It brings me such peace just watching my plants grow.

I took a look at my Instagram and realized the accounts I followed made my page account full of negativity. Negative things such as friends and family complaining about unimportant first world problems, news, partying, clubbing, and poor expectations of body image. A clean-up of my page was needed and I started to only follow accounts that brought me joy, I unfollowed any page that didn't bring me peace. I started following pages that promoted healthy eating ideas, realistic ideas of body image, animals, natural products, travelling, running, exercise, meditation, ecofriendly things, and ideas and events that are world-changing, and more. From then on, when I looked at my feed, I would only see positive things. This helped me in such a positive way by focusing my energy on only things that served me.

I decided to write a list of things I wanted to accomplish. I had minor things like go to a lavender field, take a CPR course, and more drastic things such as skydiving! This list helped me look forward to something. It helped me see a clearer future and start planning things; although, I am regretting the skydiving one already! Once I outlined what I wanted out of life, I became excited.

I have always been an animal person but got even closer to my pets. They have always brought me so much joy. So, I surrounded myself with animals and nature. I took time to just be and started going for walks, walking my dogs, and listening to the birds sing.

I have always enjoyed reading books of all genres. I bought myself a bunch of books to keep myself busy. Reading helps your mind escape for a little while; it was exactly what I needed, to get away for a while.

What makes you happy?

What is on your happiness to-do list?

_____

_____

_____

_____

_____

_____

_____

_____

_____

_____

_____

_____

_____

_____

_____

_____

_____

_____

_____

_____

_____

_____

_____

_____

_____

_____

_____

Take a look at your social media, are you following any pages that do not bring you joy or self-improvement? Do you need to do a clean-up?

_____

_____

_____

_____

_____

_____

_____

_____

_____

_____

_____

_____

_____

_____

_____

_____

_____

_____

_____

_____

_____

_____

_____

_____

_____

_____

_____

_____

_____

Find something to keep you healthy: mentally and physically

The day my mom was diagnosed with cancer, I made the choice to become vegan. I cut out all animal products and have never looked back. It was a spur-of-the-moment decision but one I had thought about for a long time. My childhood friend is a vegan chef, and she helped make my transition to veganism so much easier. Any question I had about veganism, she was only a text away. Becoming a vegan was the best decision I have ever made. My skin is clearer, my nails and hair are longer, and I feel great. I am full of energy and genuinely feel happier since becoming vegan.

To clear my head, I meditated for three minutes a day. Since I have made this a part of my daily routine, I can balance my emotions better and take time for myself and my healing. My favourite thing to do is meditate in my garden and listen to the birds sing.

Every morning when I wake up and every night before I go to bed, I write in my gratitude journal. It forces me to think positive and start and end every day on a positive note. It teaches me to be grateful for my life and my memories. Optimism is contagious; if you are optimistic, it rubs off on those around you.

A fairweather runner, I would run only on spring/early summer days for short distances. Lately, I have forced myself to go out a minimum of once a week. A runner's high is a real thing. No one comes home from a run in a negative state.

I made all these life changes, hoping to achieve overall better health.

What things can you change in your life to keep yourself mentally and physically healthy?

_____

_____

_____

_____

_____

_____

_____

_____

_____

_____

_____

_____

_____

_____

_____

_____

_____

_____

_____

_____

_____

_____

_____

_____

_____

_____

_____

_____

How can you recharge and balance your emotions better?

_____

_____

_____

_____

_____

_____

_____

_____

_____

_____

_____

_____

_____

_____

_____

_____

_____

_____

_____

_____

_____

_____

_____

_____

_____

_____

_____

Find something to keep you busy

After going through such trauma, the worst thing I could do was sit still and think. I needed to keep myself busy. On a particularly hard day, I decided to write an email to my dad. I went on a very heartfelt rant, thanking him for everything he had ever done for me. In my email, I asked him to send me something to help me move forward. I also told him that I would honour him and make him proud of me. Almost instantly upon concluding my email, it came to me! I was going to do a memorial 15 km run for him and call it Rick's Run. All funds collected would go directly to the Heart & Stroke Foundation. I quickly went online and opened a Go Fund Me Account to start fundraising. My original goal was to raise $6,000; I surpassed that within a month. My new goal was $10,000. I didn't expect to have people want to join, but I received an overwhelming response. I had over sixty people sign up to run, walk or bike. I had people running from Toronto, Quebec, Ireland, and British Columbia! I also had a vendor from work offer to make me and all the runners' Tshirts. I had my Go Fund Me post shared on Facebook by Tom Cochrane!

It seems people love it when a person takes a negative situation and turns it into something positive. My dad was so well respected, it didn't take much to reach our goal. As this happened during Covid-19, to promote social distancing, all runners had to run from a location of their choice. As a team, we managed to raise $30,000 CAD total! I also had a section on Rick's Run broadcasted on Global News! The Global News segment helped me realize my love for speaking! The segment inspired me to share my story. Next time, I hope to have this run from one specific location so we can all honour my dad together. This will be an annual event for me, each year with a higher goal amount. By organizing this, I was keeping busy while honouring my dad at the same time! For more information on Rick's Run and how you can get involved, visit my Instagram page @jamiesokoloff.

Writing this book has been an amazing way to keep busy while still honouring my dad! I have never been one to speak to others about my life experiences, but I realized that his influence on me needed to be shared and reach as many people as possible. I hope to help people cope with loss and get their lives back on track. This book started off as free therapy for me. Writing my story has made me feel better, a literal release of my feelings. When life throws a curveball (or multiple curveballs in my case), how you react is crucial. Since childhood, I have been a huge book lover and have read hundreds of books throughout my twenty-seven years. Writing always came naturally to me, especially when writing about something that I was passionate about. So, *Persevering for Peace* has held me accountable to every piece of advice I have given and forced me to practice what I preach.

At this point in my life, I was restless. I needed something new and exciting to keep me motivated but also something to make me more money. I decided to open Air & Water Naturals as a small side business, which offers handmade natural products ranging from infused olive oils to bath crystals. I am a huge believer in using all natural products and had so many essential oils around my house that I found a way to use them! I began making these products for fun but decided that I could actually make some money and share my natural creations with others. I set up a small Instagram shop and sold a few items to friends. The meaning of "air and water" is simple. My element sign is air and my dad's was water. Through this little business, I was, again, keeping busy while honouring my dad's spirit.

What things can you do to keep yourself busy while being successful at the same time?

_____

_____

_____

_____

_____

_____

_____

_____

_____

_____

_____

_____

_____

_____

_____

_____

_____

_____

_____

_____

_____

_____

_____

_____

_____

_____

_____

_____

Give yourself alone time

Throughout this tragic time, I found myself helping others dealing with their own pain. I focused my energy on others, wanting to help them instead of dealing with my own grief. I didn't take enough time for my own healing. As I helped others with their grief, I absorbed their pain and energy and added to mine. I realized that I was being empathic.

When hearing others' problems or getting involved in issues that had nothing to do with me, I became sensitive and sad. I wanted to help others and avoid dealing with my own issues. I took on other people's energy but was unaware that I was doing it. I always needed to recharge after being with others for long periods of time and never understood why.

Once I realized that I was an empath, I knew that I needed to protect my energy, to provide space for myself to heal and time to process my grief, and look inward. I started doing things alone, going for walks, journaling, reading, trying Reiki sessions, and focusing on my healing. After listening to someone else's issues, I needed to take a step back and let go of their energy. In other words, to leave things at the door and not take them home with me. In college, a professor told me the best way not to burn out was to pick a tree on the way out of anywhere you go and decide to leave everything negative from the day at the tree. Once you leave all the problems and emotions of the day there, you could end your day with a different mindset. It teaches you to balance your energy and to avoid retaining negative energy from others.

I learned to recharge and take space for myself. I learned to assist without taking on their emotions as my own. Space is the greatest gift as it allows for time to focus on your pain and emotions. I find someday even fifteen minutes of alone time does so much good for me. If I am stressed out or angry with someone, I know now to take a step back and give myself solitude to recharge. After a fifteenminute break, I am then able to come back to the situation in a different frame of mind.

I have learned throughout my healing journey to listen to my intuition. When my parents left for their trip to Tahiti, a sense of sadness came over me and I needed to give my dad a big hug and tell him I loved him. I didn't know why I felt like that, as they travelled often, but I know now that it was my intuition telling me to say goodbye. A few months after my dad had passed, my mom was heading to their cottage to be with some friends. When she left, I had a terrible feeling in my stomach and knew something bad was going to happen. I called her often that weekend to check in with her, still not sharing my bad feeling. Later that weekend, I got a call from my mom; I knew before I answered her call that something bad had happened. She said her dog had fallen off of the dock and into the lake and drowned. She called me, panicked, but while I was on the phone with her, her friend revived him by pressing on his stomach to remove the water from his lungs. Thank our lucky stars the dog recovered quickly. Listening to your intuition is a surefire way to judge a situation and make decisions. I learned to trust my gut more and listen to my inner voice.

How can you manage to take some alone time? What would you do with this time?

Reading, exercising, writing, meditating?

_____

_____

_____

_____

_____

_____

_____

_____

_____

_____

_____

_____

_____

_____

_____

_____

_____

_____

_____

_____

_____

_____

_____

_____

_____

_____

_____

_____

Attitude is EVERYTHING!

When I decided to move forward with my life and live for my dad, it was extremely hard to stay positive. I struggled with my emotions and broke into tears often. I caught myself being negative and focusing on the bad. When I realized that my emotions were 100% my choice, I pulled myself out of negative thinking quicker. Once I balanced them and gained control, good things started happening. I started attracting opportunities and experiences that I never thought were possible. When you gain control and think positive thoughts, you attract good things. When you focus your energy on the positive, your outlook starts to change, and you open yourself up to more beautiful things to attract into your life.

Attitude is the most important thing. When you choose love and peace, you attract love and peace. When you choose hate and anger, guess what you attract?

If you are angry, find out what is making you angry. Move away from the things that anger you and focus on what brings you joy. When you can determine what is triggering your negative emotions, you are able to eliminate these things from your life. Is a conversation angering you? Change the topic! Is the news making you depressed? Change the channel! You are in control of yourself.

Make a promise to yourself to focus on the positive and put less energy into the negative. Put your energy into making a positive difference and bringing yourself joy, and I guarantee you will attract a life that makes you happy.

What makes you angry? How can you focus less energy on this?

_____

_____

_____

_____

_____

_____

_____

_____

_____

_____

_____

_____

_____

_____

_____

_____

_____

_____

_____

_____

_____

_____

_____

_____

_____

_____

_____

What makes you positive? How can you put more energy into this?

_____

_____

_____

_____

_____

_____

_____

_____

_____

_____

_____

_____

_____

_____

_____

_____

_____

_____

_____

_____

_____

_____

_____

_____

_____

_____

_____

Final Self-Reflection Exercise

As you reach the end of this guide, please take this opportunity on the next few pages, to reflect on what you have learned and how you will apply it to your own life. Think deep and allow time for deep reflection. I wish you a life full of happiness, love and purpose. It has been an honour to share this journey with you and I hope my story of self-development and healing brings you peace in some way or another. I hope my father's life lessons can be a positive light on your journey to peace, as they have been on mine.

Xoxo, Jamie

What takeaways from this book will you apply to your life?

_____
_____
_____
_____
_____
_____
_____
_____
_____
_____
_____
_____
_____
_____
_____
_____
_____
_____
_____
_____
_____
_____
_____
_____
_____
_____
_____
_____

What life changes do you need to make to live a more fulfilling, happy life?

_____
_____
_____
_____
_____
_____
_____
_____
_____
_____
_____
_____
_____
_____
_____
_____
_____
_____
_____
_____
_____
_____
_____
_____
_____
_____

Who do you want to be? How can you become the best version of yourself?

_____

_____

_____

_____

_____

_____

_____

_____

_____

_____

_____

_____

_____

_____

_____

_____

_____

_____

_____

_____

_____

_____

_____

_____

_____

_____

_____

_____

*How can you remember to enjoy every day? What do
you need to add to your daily routine to hold yourself
accountable for choosing happiness?*

Who is the most memorable person in your life (living or otherwise)? What lessons have you learned from this person? How can you apply these lessons to your own life? Who can you reach out to for support? A friend, family member, life coach, sibling?

_____

_____

_____

_____

_____

_____

_____

_____

_____

_____

_____

_____

_____

_____

_____

_____

_____

_____

_____

_____

_____

_____

_____

_____

_____

What values do you have? What is important to you?

_____

_____

_____

_____

_____

_____

_____

_____

_____

_____

_____

_____

_____

_____

_____

_____

_____

_____

_____

_____

_____

_____

_____

_____

_____

_____

_____

_____

_____

_____

_____

How can you help others? How does helping others make you feel?

What is the best thing to ever happen to you?

_____

_____

_____

_____

_____

_____

_____

_____

_____

_____

_____

_____

_____

_____

_____

_____

_____

_____

_____

_____

_____

_____

_____

_____

_____

_____

What is the worst thing to ever happen to you and how did you grow from it?

_____

_____

_____

_____

_____

_____

_____

_____

_____

_____

_____

_____

_____

_____

_____

_____

_____

_____

_____

_____

_____

_____

_____

_____

_____

_____

_____

What do you want out of life? What are your goals?
What does your dream life look like?

_____

_____

_____

_____

_____

_____

_____

_____

_____

_____

_____

_____

_____

_____

_____

_____

_____

_____

_____

_____

_____

_____

_____

_____

_____

Your goal list and how you can make yourself accountable. (This can be as small or as big as you would like it to be!)

Goal	What steps are you taking to achieve this?	Approximate completion date	Completed (Hell...yeah!)
e.g. Run a Marathon	- Joined a running club - I do not go more than 3 days without going for a run - Chose a goal race several months from now - Found an accountability buddy to help me achieve my goal - Set monthly distance goals	- 6 months from today - Race Day is August 2021	YES!!!!!
Goal #1			
Goal #2			
Goal # 3			

Where do you want to be next year? What steps do you need to take to get there?

_____

_____

_____

_____

_____

_____

_____

_____

_____

_____

_____

_____

_____

_____

_____

_____

_____

_____

_____

_____

_____

_____

_____

_____

_____

_____

_____

What does it mean to you to persevere?

_____

_____

_____

_____

_____

_____

_____

_____

_____

_____

_____

_____

_____

_____

_____

_____

_____

_____

_____

_____

_____

_____

_____

_____

_____

_____

_____

_____

How can you see the big picture in life and live your dream?

_____

_____

_____

_____

_____

_____

_____

_____

_____

_____

_____

_____

_____

_____

_____

_____

_____

_____

_____

_____

_____

_____

_____

_____

_____

_____

What is your purpose in life?

_____

_____

_____

_____

_____

_____

_____

_____

_____

_____

_____

_____

_____

_____

_____

_____

_____

_____

_____

_____

_____

_____

_____

_____

_____

_____

_____

_____

_____

What do you want to be remembered for? What is your legacy?

_____

_____

_____

_____

_____

_____

_____

_____

_____

_____

_____

_____

_____

_____

_____

_____

_____

_____

_____

_____

_____

_____

_____

_____

_____

_____

_____

_____

_____

Write down five things about yourself that you would like to improve on:

1.

2.

3.

4.

5.

How can you begin to improve on these things?

_____
_____
_____
_____
_____
_____
_____
_____
_____
_____
_____
_____
_____
_____
_____
_____

Write down five things you love about yourself:

    1.

    2.

    3.

    4.

    5.

What are your talents?

_____

_____

_____

_____

_____

_____

_____

_____

_____

_____

_____

_____

_____

_____

_____

_____

_____

_____

What do you bring to the world?

_____

_____

_____

_____

_____

_____

_____

_____

_____

_____

_____

_____

_____

_____

_____

_____

_____

_____

_____

_____

_____

_____

_____

_____

_____

_____

_____

_____

Write down affirmations for yourself and transfer them to a note on your phone, look at these daily to remind yourself why you are here and what you bring to the world.

I am caring.

I am kind.

I am loyal.

I am strong

A Toast to Dad

This is the eulogy I gave at my dad's funeral. It is raw and emotional and truly captures how I felt about my dad. I am proud of this speech as this was a moment that I truly felt my dad's strength within me the most. I have never written truer words than these:

Before I start, I need you all to understand that this is the hardest thing I have ever had to do in my whole life so please bear with me.

I want you all to close your eyes and think of your favourite person in the world who always has your back. When I close my eyes, I see my dad. He was my everything.

My dad was the best father Steve and I could have ever imagined. He was supportive and loved us to no ends no matter what we did. He was proud of his family.

My dad built an empire from the ground up and worked so hard his entire life but not once do I remember my dad not being there throughout our childhood. We were his main priority.

He would've done anything for us and was always just a call away. I could call him for directions, for advice, when I was angry, when a strange light would turn on in my car, when I was sad, when I missed a flight, the list goes on. Whatever I needed, he was there, always, no matter what time it was or where in the world he was.

Steve and I were so fortunate to work with our dad for many years. He let us make our own judgement calls and would always be there to back us up. No matter what, he had our back. Steve, I know you will make Dad proud and make Quality soar to the top.

My dad would call me every Friday at work just to check in. He mainly wanted to talk about life and let me know what he and my mom were up to. Romeo would always be squeaking a toy in the background and he would laugh and tell me that Romeo was sitting on his lap.

Him and I had an unbreakable bond that was sometimes intertwined with tough love. He called me out when I was wrong and told me when I needed to toughen up. He wanted me to see the big picture in life and not sweat the small stuff. After one particular fight in my previous relationship, I was sad and upset and he said "Jamie enough of this. Stop feeling sorry for yourself and get your life together." So I did. I moved on with my life and didn't look back. Which lead me to meet the love of my life, Jesse. My dad made me feel confident, like I could accomplish anything in the world. I was Daddy's little girl and he always told me that no matter how old him and I got, I would always be his baby.

My dad and I always bonded on the "Sokoloff luck". We would always talk about how fortunate we were, how much good we had. How good life could be. He told me how much he enjoyed his life and loved my mom. When we went through bad times, him and I would always try to find a positive in every situation. so here I am in a bad situation, trying to find the positive in this. After racking my brain, I found it. We all were so incredibly fortunate to have my dad in our lives. He made us strong, resilient, and generous. The positive of this is that I got to know what true love is from the first man to ever love me. I got to have a positive example in my life.

Whether it was through business, his BBQing and teppenyaki skills, boating or cottaging, from the amount of people here today, I can see that he had quite the impact on everyone he met.

I understood him and he understood me. He was so proud of me and Steve. He never compared us, he was just equally proud and honoured to have us as his children. And he was so thrilled to have a granddaughter on the way. Jesse and Maria, he loved you both too like his own. He was so happy that Steve and I had someone to support us and enjoy life with. He was honoured to have us all in his presence. Well, guess what, Dad, the pleasure was all ours.

We will use his strong will and excellent example to do good for this world. He would not want us to feel sorry for ourselves and would want us to move forward and use our negative experience as positive life lessons. I will miss his quirks and the fact that he always had to have slippers on his feet.

When life got us down, I could always count on my dad to make me smile. His smile was contagious. He had certain sayings that will always ring in my head. Whenever he opened a fortune cookie he would say, "He who gets hit by car has run down feelings." There are so many more of them, I could be here all day.

My favourite memories with him were the cottage weekends he would cook for us and ensure we were always well fed and build a great big bonfire where we would talk and have some drinks together and look out into the water. He and I would talk about life and the future. I will always remember our daddydaughter dance at the end of Casper. I can't count how many times I would step on his feet and dance with him to the closing song. I always enjoyed our walks with the dogs, they were peaceful, and we really bonded over them.

My dad was the grill master, he would cook for everyone, and at one point he cooked chicken wings for over ninety people at his cottage party. He loved to cook and made sure everyone was fed and had a drink in their hand.

He loved animals and I think I got that trait from him. He loved feeding birds. He loved boating, fishing, America's Got Talent, the outdoors, our pets, snacks, and most of all, my mom.

My mom was the absolute love of his life, besides Romeo. She was his rock and he would go through the end of the earth for her. He loved her with all his heart and showed it every day. Their love story is one for the books and Dad, I will never forget the way you looked at Mom. You showed me what love is. I will never forget how his eyes lit up when talking about my mom. Together since they were fifteen, they were inseparable. Most people do not get this kind of love in their lifetime.

It was an absolute pleasure to have you as a dad and I am forever grateful for our bond and final moments together. I gave you a big hug and told you I loved you and I am so truly grateful to remember you like this.

I only hope that I can be as good of an example to my kids as you were to us. Let this be a reminder to us all how short life can be. My dad loved every minute that he was on this earth and for that I am eternally grateful.

Until we *meet again my sweet daddy, I will make* you *proud, I promise* you *that.* You *will live on in* your *legacy. I will miss* you *forever. But I will live my life and see the beauty in the world again just like* you *would want me to. Thank* you *for the life* you *gave us I am forever grateful for it and I will never forget to appreciate my life. To all of* you *please live* your *life to the fullest and love each other unconditionally. Life is too short to sweat the small stuff and my dad always tried to tell me that. As my dad would say, just keep persevering.*

Love you *always Daddy, I will forever be* your *baby girl.*

Into the Water; You Must Go

Into the water you must go,
Your heart and soul have escaped you
and lead you to somewhere new.
The memories will remain in our hearts forever
Our love for you will not fade not now, not ever.

Thank you for this beautiful life, your wisdom and that
infectious smile
I wish you could've stayed, even for just a little while
It never would've been long enough,
But one more hug would do.

I knew my heart would break one day, but I never
thought this soon.
As I walk through life, without you,
I know I will make it through
Because you are my sun and all of my stars,
Your presence is everywhere and I know you are
never far

As I walk on this journey of life without you
I remember your smile and your laugh
And smile at all of our memories and sometimes cry too.

Although the tears flow often
I am so grateful for the time spent together
These memories will last forever
You are my world, you are my moon.

For when I am feeling sad, for when I am missing you
Down to the water I will go and allow the memories
of you to flow